PRAYERS & PROMISES

for MEN

BroadStreet
PUBLISHING

CONTENTS

INTRODUCTION

It is a wonderful blessing to be a son of God! You can take great joy in knowing that he made you for a purpose and he desires a close relationship with you. Spending time in his Word each day will fill you with strength, wisdom, and peace.

Prayers & Promises for Men incorporates more than 70 themes to help you receive inspiration found in the promises of God's Word. Uplifting prayers offer the opportunity for deeper reflection.

Be encouraged and strengthened as you dwell on the faithfulness of God.

ABANDONMENT

"The Lord himself goes before you and will be with you;
he will never leave you nor forsake you."

Deuteronomy 31:8 NIV

The Lord loves justice and fairness;
he will never abandon his people.
They will be kept safe forever.

Psalm 37:28 TLB

God makes a home for the lonely;
He leads out the prisoners into prosperity.

Psalm 68:6 NASB

"I will not abandon you as orphans—
I will come to you."

John 14:18 NLT

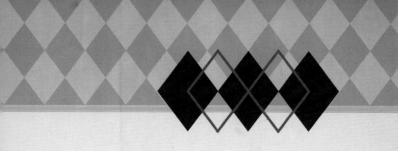

Father, you are faithful and true to your promises. Help me remember the times you stood by me and renewed my strength when I thought no one supported me. Teach me of the other men you have stood beside in times of loneliness and struggle—like David, Moses, and Jesus—so I am strengthened against my fears. Remind me once again of your certain promise to restore and fulfill so I may overcome this trial with the joy of victory that you will bring with you.

**Do you truly believe that
God will never leave you?**

ACCEPTANCE

"The Father gives me the people who are mine.
Every one of them will come to me,
and I will always accept them."

JOHN 6:37 NCV

The LORD does not see as man sees;
for man looks at the outward appearance,
but the LORD looks at the heart.

1 SAMUEL 16:7 NKJV

Before he made the world,
God chose us to be his very own
through what Christ would do for us; he decided then
to make us holy in his eyes, without a single fault—
we who stand before him covered with his love.

EPHESIANS 1:4 TLB

My Lord, you are awesome and majestic, amazing in your ways! You invite me to your table as one of your companions, as David with his men, and you strengthen me with your kindness. You are not ashamed to confront me in my failings and call me to stand and own myself before you, but you stand with me. You strengthen me by your companionship and willingness to call me to go with you in the mission you have set before me: to empower others to stand true to the day of your restoration. You are a good friend.

How does God's acceptance of you help you to be more accepting of others?

ADOPTION

You did not receive a spirit of slavery to fall back into fear,
but you have received a spirit of adoption.
When we cry, "Abba! Father!" it is that very Spirit
bearing witness with our spirit
that we are children of God.

ROMANS 8:15–16 NRSV

A father of the fatherless and a judge for the widows,
Is God in His holy habitation.
God makes a home for the lonely;
He leads out the prisoners into prosperity.

PSALM 68:5-6 NASB

The LORD will not abandon His people
on account of His great name,
because the LORD has been pleased
to make you a people for Himself.

1 SAMUEL 12:22 NASB

My Father, I am humbled you have drawn me to yourself and made me one of your own. I have been a lonely wanderer, hoping to find my way and purpose in this life, struggling with feeling unworthy if I haven't made a name for myself. You, however, have given me a name and have made me a part of the grandest story. You have freely offered me a place in your family though my roots have been founded in rebellion. I am your son, and you are my Father, and all of this according to your own desire. I glorify you!

How does knowing that God has adopted you into his family make you feel?

ANXIETY

You will keep in perfect peace those whose
minds are steadfast, because they trust in you.

ISAIAH 26:3 NIV

"Don't let your hearts be troubled.
Trust in God, and trust also in me."

JOHN 14:1 NLT

Give all your worries to him,
because he cares about you.

1 PETER 5:7 NCV

I call out to the LORD when I'm in trouble,
and he answers me.

PSALM 120:1 NIRV

O Mighty King, your promises are true and certain because you have the power and authority to make them true. You have shown your faithfulness to your Word throughout the story of life; you have established your people and continue to draw each of us to yourself. You have promised that you will restore and replenish the earth, and you will refresh our souls with newness of breath. I can rest steadfastly in your promises, my strong tower, for you do not lie. I am filled with joy in times of trouble because of your Word. You fill me with courage by your Holy Spirit.

What steps can you take to be less anxious and more trusting?

ASSURANCE

To him who is able to do immeasurably more
than all we ask or imagine, according to his power
that is at work within us, to him be glory...
for ever and ever! Amen.

EPHESIANS 3:20–21 NIV

All of God's promises have been fulfilled
in Christ with a resounding "Yes!"

2 CORINTHIANS 1:20 NLT

Jesus Christ is the same yesterday and today and forever.

HEBREWS 13:8 NASB

These things I have written to you who believe
in the name of the Son of God, that you may know
that you have eternal life, and that you may
continue to believe in the name of the Son of God.

1 JOHN 5:13 NKJV

Kind Father, I am uncertain and need encouragement. You have set forth your promises and are faithful to fulfill what you have determined. However, my eyes are weak, and I do not always see. Fill me with your Holy Spirit and remind me of your great works of old, so I may be encouraged to hold confident assurance in you and in the plans you have established. Then, I will be able to reside confidently in the certainty of faith, assured of your work. May my faith be fully rooted in your promises, and may I not be comforted by my own hopes and dreams but be built up in the truth of your great calling. I stand on your firm foundations, magnificent God.

How does believing God's promises cause you to feel reassured?

BELIEF

If you instruct the brethren in these things,
you will be a good minister of Jesus Christ,
nourished in the words of faith and of the
good doctrine which you have carefully followed.

1 TIMOTHY 4:6 NKJV

To all who did accept him and believe in him
he gave the right to become children of God.

JOHN 1:12 NCV

"All things are possible to him who believes."

MARK 9:23 NASB

"Have you believed because you have seen me?
Blessed are those who have not seen
and yet have believed."

JOHN 20:29 ESV

I believe you, Lord my God, and the firmness of your will. I put my faith in you that you have established your creation according to your plan, and according to that same will you will restore all who put their trust in you. I am strengthened by the message of your power and the good news of redemption you have established through Jesus' first coming. Merciful One, I pray that you will strengthen me against my unbelief, in those times when my focus drops from the certainty of you and is drawn away to the wayward circumstances of this life that war against my believing in your promised redemption. Act in accordance with the power of your Holy Spirit to strengthen my belief in you and the power you will exert to fulfill your great redemptive promise.

How can you strengthen your belief in God?

BLESSINGS

Surely, Lord, you bless those who do what is right.
Like a shield, your loving care keeps them safe.

PSALM 5:12 NIRV

Surely you have granted him unending blessings
and made him glad with the joy of your presence.

PSALM 21:6 NIV

Give praise to the God and Father of our Lord Jesus Christ.
He has blessed us with every spiritual blessing.
Those blessings come from the heavenly world.
They belong to us because we belong to Christ.
God chose us to belong to Christ
before the world was created.
He chose us to be holy and without blame in his eyes.
He loved us.

EPHESIANS 1:3-4 NIRV

Thank you, Lord, for the greatness of the gifts you bestow on those who trust in you and believe you for their deliverance. You are liberal in your generosity, blessing your people with everlasting life and enduring provision. My cup overflows! Strengthen my hands in doing what is right and good that my conscience may remain clear and the faithful assurance of your Word will produce blessing even greater than I could hope or imagine. Set my heart and my eyes on the great hope of blessing that you bring with you at the great day of your majesty.

Which of God's blessings can you thank him for today?

BOLDNESS

He proclaimed the kingdom of God
and taught about the Lord Jesus Christ—
with all boldness and without hindrance!

ACTS 28:31 NIV

Sinners run away even when no one is chasing them.
But those who do what is right are as bold as lions.

PROVERBS 28:1 NIRV

On the day I called you, you answered me.
You made me strong and brave.

PSALM 138:3 NCV

Let us come boldly to the throne of our gracious God.
There we will receive his mercy,
and we will find grace to help us when we need it most.

HEBREWS 4:16 NLT

My Comforter, I need you to embolden my weak heart. By your great Spirit and the certainty of your gospel promises, I may stand with strength in the face of adversity and trial, but I am weak by myself and in my own confidence. I trust in you for boldness and certainty of conviction: certainty that your way and promises are good and true, worthy to be declared and to stand firmly for them. In the face of a world that roars against your precepts, strengthen me to root myself in your promises and I will stand true in boldness for the graciousness of your good news.

How do you find courage to be both bold and tenderhearted?

CHANGE

Look! I tell you this secret:
We will not all sleep in death,
but we will all be changed.

1 CORINTHIANS 15:51 NCV

He will take our weak mortal bodies
and change them into glorious bodies like his own,
using the same power with which he will bring
everything under his control.

PHILIPPIANS 3:21 NLT

Jesus Christ is the same
yesterday and today and forever.

HEBREWS 13:8 NIRV

Lord, you are like a rock in its steadiness and strength. I can stand firm on the stable foundation you set by your unchanging ways. When I need to set my ways in truth, I can trust in the standard you have established, for you do not shift like sand. You have promised me a sure foundation that will steady me against the waywardness of my own heart. I confess that I am too easily swayed by things in this life, and all too often I change and am molded by the pressures of life, family, or friends. You provide me a firm hand that molds me into your very own character, and what's more, you will solidify me by the power of your resurrection at the day of your coming.

How do you handle change?

COMFORT

May our Lord Jesus Christ himself and God our Father,
who loved us and by his grace gave us
eternal comfort and a wonderful hope,
comfort you and strengthen you.

2 THESSALONIANS 2:16–17 NLT

Unless the LORD had helped me,
I would soon have settled in the silence of the grave.
I cried out, "I am slipping!"
but your unfailing love, O LORD, supported me.
When doubts filled my mind,
your comfort gave me renewed hope and cheer.

PSALM 94:17–19 NLT

To all who mourn he will give: beauty for ashes;
joy instead of mourning; praise instead of heaviness.
For God has planted them like strong and
graceful oaks for his own glory.

ISAIAH 61:3 TLB

*Father, your Word has established that you will not leave
me as an orphan, but that you will come to me and reside
with me forever. Multiple times your Word declares that your
dwelling will be right here on the earth amongst humanity.
You will comfort us from the death cycle of this age and
sustain us with everlasting life. My great God, how I need
the comfort of that message today! Remind me through the
power of your Holy Spirit of the greatness of the reward that
is coming so I may be comforted. My heart breaks from the
things I see and the pain that surrounds me. Redeem your
people and fulfill the promises you have made so we may rest
in your great peace.*

Do you feel the comforting presence
of God today?

CONFIDENCE

I can do everything through Christ,
who gives me strength.

PHILIPPIANS 4:13 NLT

Be my rock of refuge,
to which I can always go;
give the command to save me,
for you are my rock and my fortress....
For You have been my hope, Sovereign LORD,
my confidence since my youth.

PSALM 71:3, 5 NIV

Do not throw away your confidence,
which has a great reward.

HEBREWS 10:35 NCV

When the things of this life attempt to entice me into trusting in them for my own benefit and comfort, your faithful promises, God, give me confidence that true life comes only through you. I can certainly withstand the temptations of this age and the fleeting benefits of this life because of the everlasting hope of your promised redemption. You strengthen me by this message, and in this assurance, I put my confidence. Thank you for standing firm as my powerful captain and my rear guard, giving me confidence to strive for the reward that is coming.

How do you find your confidence in God?

CONTENTMENT

To enjoy your work and to accept your lot in life—
that is indeed a gift from God.
The person who does that
will not need to look back with sorrow on his past,
for God gives him joy.

ECCLESIASTES 5:20 TLB

I know what it is to be in need,
and I know what it is to have plenty.
I have learned the secret of being content
in any and every situation,
whether well fed or hungry,
whether living in plenty or in want.
I can do all this through him who gives me strength.

PHILIPPIANS 4:12–13 NIV

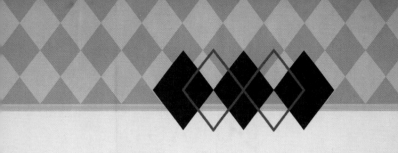

Father, my heart longs for more, to be someone of stature, to have something I can call my own. I am tempted to seek after things I think will satisfy me, but I also know that the satisfaction they produce lasts far too short a time. Remind me of the goodness of your promises and how plentiful they will be, and I can turn from life's temptations and be content with what I have in this life. When I set my sights on the greater reward you have declared from the beginning, I am satisfied regardless of my current circumstances. I pray that you will strengthen me by this to live righteously so in the day of reward I will not be ashamed.

How can you choose to be content with life as it is right now?

COURAGE

Be strong in the Lord and in his mighty power.
Put on the full armor of God, so that you can
take your stand against the devil's schemes.

EPHESIANS 6:10-11 NIV

Be alert. Continue strong in the faith.
Have courage, and be strong. Do everything in love.

1 CORINTHIANS 16:13-14 NCV

Even though I walk through the darkest valley,
I will not be afraid. You are with me.
Your shepherd's rod and staff comfort me.

PSALM 23:4 NIRV

"This is my command—be strong and courageous!
Do not be afraid or discouraged.
For the LORD your God is with you wherever you go."

JOSHUA 1:9 NLT

Father, I fear the pain and hard trials of this life. My body shrinks back from the difficulties that often accompany living for your reward and commendation. Strengthen me by your Holy Spirit to stand firm in the midst of my fear that swirls around me and enable me to drink from the cup you have set before me. You strengthened Jesus by the certainty of the great promises you established, and he was able to face his fear with confidence that a crown awaited him. May I follow also in his footsteps and remember your redemption so I don't follow my fear but am filled with courage to overcome. I thank you that you provide the means of this courage.

When was the last time you asked God for courage?

DELIGHT

When I received your words, I ate them.
They filled me with joy. My heart took delight in them.
LORD God who rules over all, I belong to you.

JEREMIAH 15:16 NIRV

"My God, I want to do what you want.
Your teachings are in my heart."

PSALM 40:8 NCV

Your laws are my treasure;
they are my heart's delight.

PSALM 119:111 NLT

"Let your light shine before others, that they may see
your good deeds and glorify your Father in heaven."

MATTHEW 5:16 NIV

Your mercy and goodness, O Lord, are delightful. I am amazed by your Word of truth. You fill me with excitement at the thought of your promises and work, and I am glad to follow the path you have established. Your ways are full of wisdom and lead to great joy. It delights me to reveal your good news to others—to magnify the path to life that your Word illuminates. May my heart delight in your way and may I be rewarded in your presence as you have declared.

How do you realize God's incredible delight?

DELIVERANCE

I waited patiently for the LORD;

he turned to me and heard my cry.

He lifted me out of the slimy pit,

out of the mud and mire;

he set my feet on a rock

and gave me a firm place to stand.

He put a new song in my mouth,

a hymn of praise to our God.

Many will see and fear the LORD;

and put their trust in him.

PSALM 40:1–3 NIV

Humble yourselves in the sight of the Lord,

and He will lift you up.

JAMES 4:10 NKJV

The righteous person faces many troubles,

but the LORD comes to the rescue each time.

PSALM 34:19 NLT

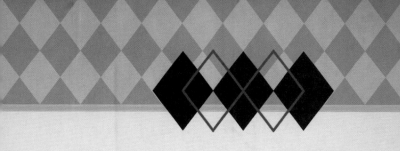

Deliver me, my Father, from the hands of the enemy who wishes to see me despair. Give me peace in the depths of my heart and let me not falter. Restore to me the joy of the knowledge of your salvation. Reinforce the truth of your redemption and comfort me in your great mercy. You are a friend to the humble and downtrodden, restoring their lives and exalting them. I need you now. Your deliverance is assured; fill me with fresh understanding of your great strength.

Can you ask God for deliverance from your fears?

DEPRESSION

The LORD hears his people when they call to him for help.
He rescues them from all their troubles.

PSALM 34:17 NLT

Why am I so sad? Why am I so upset?
I should put my hope in God
and keep praising him.

PSALM 42:11 NCV

You, O LORD, are a shield about me,
my glory, and the lifter of my head.

PSALM 3:3 ESV

He has delivered us from the power of darkness
and conveyed us into the kingdom of the Son of His love.

COLOSSIANS 1:13 NKJV

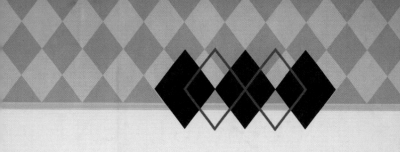

Merciful God, my heart cries out within me, yet my voice fails. Darkness seems to surround me, and the light has fled from me. I need you in this dark hour, but you seem so far away. Remind me of your promises. Let your Holy Spirit show your strength to lift my soul from gloom and darkness and restore to me the joy of life. How long, Lord, must I wait? You are patient and kind in your ways. You do not forget me here. May I exult again in the miracle of your deliverance and restoration. Fill me with the light of your good news. I will live, and my eyes will be filled with the light of your presence all the days of my life.

**Can you sense God's comfort and joy
in the middle of your sadness?**

ENCOURAGEMENT

The LORD your God is with you;
the mighty One will save you.
He will rejoice over you. You will rest in his love;
he will sing and be joyful about you.

ZEPHANIAH 3:17 NCV

Encourage one another daily,
as long as it is called "Today."

HEBREWS 3:13 NIV

Kind words are like honey—
sweet to the soul and healthy for the body.

PROVERBS 16:24 NLT

Be joyful. Grow to maturity. Encourage each other.
Live in harmony and peace. Then the God of love and
peace will be with you.

2 CORINTHIANS 13:11 NLT

Even in my weakest times you fill me, my God, with your Holy Spirit. My courage is restored by the revelation of your promises and truth. I can stand again even when the enemy surrounds me, and the joy of your salvation springs forth from my lips as a war cry of victory! No longer will the accusing words of the enemy put me to shame, for I trust in the greatness of your Word of truth. You stand as my guard, and I have been encouraged by your strength and sustaining mercy. Guide my hands into righteousness for your name's sake.

How can you find encouragement today?

ETERNITY

We are citizens of heaven,
where the Lord Jesus Christ lives.
And we are eagerly waiting for him
to return as our Savior.

PHILIPPIANS 3:20 NLT

"And if I go and prepare a place for you,
I will come back and take you to be with me
that you also may be where I am."

JOHN 14:3 NIV

That will happen in a flash,
as quickly as you can wink an eye.
It will happen at the blast of the last trumpet.
Then the dead will be raised to live forever.
And we will be changed.

1 CORINTHIANS 15:52 NIRV

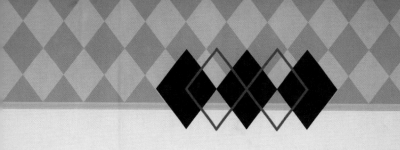

My Lord, your promises are everlasting. From age to age you stay the same. You have set our hopes in a lasting future, an inheritance without end. May your kingdom come, and your will be done here on the earth as in the heavens. I long to see your face and be filled with the confidence of your presence; may my body be strengthened by your breath of life. I am encouraged in remembering the steadfastness of your declarations. I look to the day when your table is set before me, when the waters flow in desert places, and when the produce of your kingdom fills the storehouses of the world.

Can you view eternity with a hopeful, happy heart, fully trusting in a good God?

FAITH

Through Christ you have come to trust in God.
And you have placed your faith and hope in God
because he raised Christ from the dead
and gave him great glory.

1 PETER 1:21 NLT

"Because your faith is much too small.
What I'm about to tell you is true.
If you have faith as small as a mustard seed, it is enough.
You can say to this mountain, 'Move from here to there.'
And it will move. Nothing will be impossible for you."

MATTHEW 17:20 NIRV

The important thing is faith—
the kind of faith that works through love.

GALATIANS 5:6 NCV

You have always done what you have said you would do,
Father, and so your Word can be believed fully. I put my faith
in you and your trustworthiness. Though I do not yet see the
things you have promised to those who trust in you, I have
assurance of their coming. So, I turn from my rebellion, and I
put your love for your people before me, striving to love people
according to your promises. I know and trust that you will
make good your Word and that your enemies will be put to
shame. Father, increase my faith through demonstration and
experience so I am filled with full assurance.

What gives you faith and hope in Jesus?

FAITHFULNESS

Your lovingkindness, O LORD, extends to the heavens,
Your faithfulness reaches to the skies.

PSALM 36:5 NASB

The Lord is faithful, who will establish you
and guard you from the evil one.

2 THESSALONIANS 3:3 NKJV

LORD, you are my God;
I will exalt you and praise your name,
for in perfect faithfulness
you have done wonderful things,
things planned long ago.

ISAIAH 25:1 NIV

The word of the LORD is upright,
and all his work is done in faithfulness.

PSALM 33:4 ESV

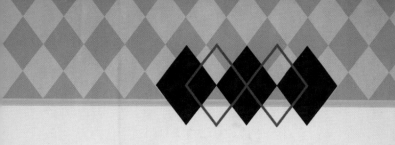

Lord, you are faithful; therefore, I need not fear my enemies. Turn my heart to you fully and cause me to trust your Word rather than the circumstances around me, so I may be found faithful to your leadership. Straighten my paths in righteousness and grace according to your great faithfulness, and I will be confident of your Word. You are good to your people whom you have redeemed; hold firm my redemption by your great mercy. I will put my trust in you because of your faithfulness. Thank you for your grace and mercy.

How have you seen the faithfulness of God played out in your life?

FEAR

God gave us his Spirit.
And the Spirit doesn't make us weak and fearful.
Instead, the Spirit gives us power and love.
He helps us control ourselves.

2 TIMOTHY 1:7 NIRV

The LORD is my light and my salvation—
whom shall I fear?
The LORD is the stronghold of my life—
of whom shall I be afraid?

PSALM 27:1 NIV

When I am afraid, I will trust you.
I praise God for his word.
I trust God, so I am not afraid.
What can human beings do to me?

PSALM 56:3-4 NCV

My Lord, I need you now. My circumstances seem too much for me, and I am afraid of what may happen. Strengthen me by your Holy Spirit, and help me overcome my fear, for I know your promises are true. Remind me in my depths of your goodness and your plans. You are my salvation and you will uphold me, regenerating my life, no matter what may happen to me. Father, thank you for keeping me in your Holy Spirit and not abandoning me to dread the things of this life.

What fears can you give to God today?

FORGIVENESS

"If you forgive other people when they sin against you,
your heavenly Father will also forgive you."

MATTHEW 6:14 NIV

Put up with each other. Forgive one another if you are
holding something against someone.
Forgive, just as the Lord forgave you.

COLOSSIANS 3:13 NIRV

He is so rich in kindness and grace
that he purchased our freedom
with the blood of his Son and forgave our sins.

EPHESIANS 1:7 NLT

How marvelous is your forgiveness, my great King! How undeserving I am to receive it. You have invited me into your family though I come from dust, and though I have lived in open rebellion against you and your ways you forgive me through the power of the sacrificed blood of Jesus. Lord, I have nothing to hold against others that even compares to what you have promised to forgive me of, so I will live at peace with my neighbor. I am pleased to follow your example and thank you for your great mercy.

Do you need to extend forgiveness to someone today?

FREEDOM

The Lord is the Spirit,
and where the Spirit of the Lord is,
there is freedom.

2 CORINTHIANS 3:17 NIV

My brothers and sisters, you were chosen to be free.
But don't use your freedom as an excuse to live
under the power of sin. Instead, serve one another in love.

GALATIANS 5:13 NIRV

"So if the Son sets you free, you are truly free."

JOHN 8:36 NLT

We have freedom now, because Christ made us free.
So stand strong. Do not change and go back
into the slavery of the law.

GALATIANS 5:1 NCV

How great are your ways, my God, and the power of your Holy Spirit within me. You give me freedom from the power of sin and strengthen me to take control of my own impulses. Because of your redemption through Jesus' sacrifice, I am not a victim. Father, keep me in your Spirit, and I will live free to observe your ways and be filled with joy at the soon return of my King!

How does it feel to be free from your sin?

FRIENDSHIP

A friend loves you all the time,
and a brother helps in time of trouble.

PROVERBS 17:17 NCV

There are "friends" who destroy each other,
but a real friend sticks closer than a brother.

PROVERBS 18:24 NLT

"Greater love has no one than this: to lay down
one's life for one's friends. You are my friends if you do
what I command. Instead, I have called you friends,
for everything that I learned from my Father I have made
known to you."

JOHN 15:13-15 NIV

"In everything, do to others
what you would want them to do to you."

MATTHEW 7:12 NIRV

How blessed it feels to be called your friend, my Lord: to be drawn near to you and invited to eat with you, to be made whole again by your sacrifice and companionship. You have stuck by me in difficult times and I remember your devotion. Strengthen me by your Holy Spirit to be a good friend to you, to follow the path you have prepared. Help me to love you as a true friend and to pass that love on to my neighbors.

What friends spur you on in your relationship with God?

GENEROSITY

Give generously to them
and do so without a grudging heart;
then because of this the LORD your God will bless you
in all your work and in everything you put your hand to.

DEUTERONOMY 15:10 NIV

Each of you should give
what you have decided in your heart to give.
You shouldn't give if you don't want to.
You shouldn't give because you are forced to.
God loves a cheerful giver.

2 CORINTHIANS 9:7 NIRV

If you help the poor, you are lending to the LORD—
and he will repay you!

PROVERBS 19:17 NLT

I am amazed at your generosity, my Father, when I remember the ways you have provided for me in every aspect of my life. My very being owes its presence to your generosity and the joy you have in creation. As I read your Word, everywhere you are free with your good gifts, even healing those who are your enemies simply because they ask of you. May I also exhibit that generosity toward others in my life. Change my heart so I love to give. Increase my faith and trust in you so I do not worry about my own provision and give without remorse.

How do you feel when you share with others?

GOODNESS

Everything God created is good, and nothing is to be
rejected if it is received with thanksgiving.

1 TIMOTHY 4:4 NIV

Taste and see that the LORD is good.
Oh, the joys of those who take refuge in him!

PSALM 34:8 NLT

My brothers and sisters,
I am sure that you are full of goodness.
I know that you have all the knowledge you need
and that you are able to teach each other.

ROMANS 15:14 NCV

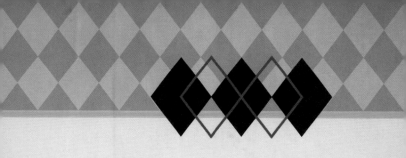

I trust you, my Father, because your ways are good and right. Even when I do not understand, I know that you have chosen what will lead to good things both for me and the whole of your creation. When I look at the circumstances of life, I do not always understand why you decree what you have or why you set in motion the activities you do, yet I know that all things work together for the good of those who are called to be conformed into your image. I trust in you and humbly seek to follow your path.

Where do you see the goodness of God most in your life?

GRACE

From his fullness we have all received,
grace upon grace.

John 1:16 NRSV

God gives us even more grace, as the Scripture says,
"God is against the proud,
but he gives grace to the humble."

James 4:6 NCV

Sin is no longer your master, for you no longer live
under the requirements of the law.
Instead, you live under the freedom of God's grace.

Romans 6:14 NLT

God, your Word states that you will give undeserved favor to those who humble themselves before you, so I ask you to continue to act favorably toward me. I recognize how proudly I have stood before you, seeking my own ways and defiantly throwing off your shackles that I thought were so confining. I thank you for your great grace, and I turn now from those things I valued so highly, for they look to be fleeting and unsatisfying in comparison to your promises. Thank you that through Jesus' sacrifice I am not subject any longer to the punishment of breaking your law, but I may freely live in accordance to your ways.

What does God's grace look like in your life?

GRATITUDE

I have not stopped giving thanks for you,
remembering you in my prayers.

EPHESIANS 1:16 NIV

Giving thanks is a sacrifice that truly honors me.
If you keep to my path,
I will reveal to you the salvation of God.

PSALM 50:23 NLT

Rejoice always, pray continually,
give thanks in all circumstances;
for this is God's will for you in Christ Jesus.

1 THESSALONIANS 5:16–18 NIV

Give thanks as you enter the gates of his temple.
Give praise as you enter its courtyards.
Give thanks to him and praise his name.

PSALM 100:4 NIRV

When I see the great works of your hands, Father, and the ways you direct the paths of the world; when I see that you have drawn your people close to you and have not left us as orphans allied with other gods and rebellious ways; when I see how you are fulfilling the promises you have made to sustain your people and make them a beacon of hope to all of us, I am filled to overflowing with joy and gratitude. I long to dance in your courts and to show you the depths of my thanks. You are good in all of your ways, my great King. I thank you!

What can you thank God for right now?

GRIEF

Those who sow in tears shall reap with shouts of joy.

PSALM 126:5 ESV

Let your steadfast love become my comfort
according to your promise to your servant.

PSALM 119:76 NRSV

"Come to me, all you who are weary and burdened,
and I will give you rest. Take my yoke upon you
and learn from me, for I am gentle and humble in heart,
and you will find rest for your souls."

MATTHEW 11:28-29 NIV

Every valley shall be raised up,
every mountain and hill made low;
the rough ground shall become level,
the rugged places a plain.

ISAIAH 40:4 NIV

My heart aches, Father, and I cannot bear the weight of this sorrow. I need the comfort only you can provide. How can I deal with the sadness and loss? Even so, your promises are of life and restoration. I need your great strength to bear up under this pain, for though I know you promise to regenerate for a short while I must withstand this loss. Father, I am not strong enough to bear the burden; stand with me or I also will succumb to the darkness. Lord, your light is a beacon to me; do not forsake me in this hour. I will stand by your great strength, and I will praise you with a willing voice because of your great comfort.

Can you ask God for help when you need his comfort?

GUIDANCE

Guide me in your truth and teach me,
for you are God my Savior,
and my hope is in you all day long.

PSALM 25:5 NIV

Wise people can also listen and learn;
even they can find good advice in these words.

PROVERBS 1:5 NCV

We can make our plans,
but the LORD determines our steps.

PROVERBS 16:9 NLT

Those who are led by the Spirit of God
are children of God.

ROMANS 8:14 NIRV

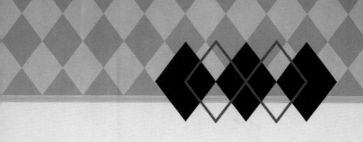

Lord, you guide me in the ways of life everlasting; I will be found in your grace. I have confidence that you lead me in truth, and that your promises will not fail. I am glad to follow your guidance because heeding your wisdom will draw me to a day of restoration and not destruction. Fill me with your Holy Spirit so I may be taught the paths of goodness and righteousness. I pledge my service to you; guide me in all of my ways.

Is there anything God can help guide you in today?

GUILT

God is faithful and fair. If we confess our sins,
he will forgive our sins. He will forgive every wrong thing
we have done. He will make us pure.

1 JOHN 1:9 NIRV

The LORD *and King helps me. He won't let me be dishonored.*
So I've made up my mind to keep on serving him.
I know he won't let me be put to shame.

ISAIAH 50:7 NIRV

Those who go to him for help are happy,
and they are never disgraced.

PSALM 34:5 NCV

I have not achieved it, but I focus on this one thing:
Forgetting the past and looking forward to
what lies ahead.

PHILIPPIANS 3:13 NLT

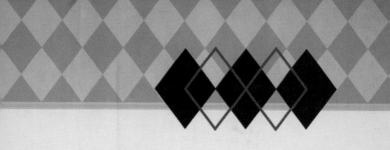

My Lord, I know the things I have done. I know how I have lived and what plans I have set thinking I would take advantage of. Yet in all of that, I was not satisfied. Then, you revealed to me your great justice. Your love knows no bounds and you are not willing to wait forever to avenge your beloved creation. You stood over me and offered redemption. Your desire is to refresh all things not destroy them. You see me in my guilt and you offer to wash me. I stand in the shower of your grace. I confess to you, and I am blessed by your cleansing of my conscience through the washing by Jesus' blood.

Why doesn't God want you to feel guilt and shame?

HEALTH

The world and its desires pass away,
but whoever does the will of God lives forever.

1 JOHN 2:17 NIV

Don't be wise in your own eyes.
Have respect for the LORD and avoid evil.
That will bring health to your body.
It will make your bones strong.

PROVERBS 3:7-8 NIRV

I will never forget your commandments,
for by them you give me life.

PSALM 119:93 NLT

A happy heart is like good medicine,
but a broken spirit drains your strength.

PROVERBS 17:22 NCV

God, you are the God of creation, the God of life, the God of restoration. You have promised to restore what you have cursed in the early days, and you will bring health and strength to the weak body I have inherited. I believe you, my King, and I ask you now to show forth your strength in healing, to refresh my soul and remind the world of your great works. For the sake of your name, I ask you to heal infirmity so that many more will glorify your name in the day of your coming. I thank you for your great gift.

What healing are you believing God for?

HONESTY

Keep me from deceitful ways;
be gracious to me and teach me your law.
I have chosen the way of faithfulness;
I have set my heart on your laws.

PSALM 119:29-30 NIV

"Everything that is hidden will become clear,
and every secret thing will be made known."

LUKE 8:17 NCV

The king is pleased with words from righteous lips;
he loves those who speak honestly.

PROVERBS 16:13 NLT

Instead, we will speak the truth in love.
So we will grow up in every way
to become the body of Christ.
Christ is the head of the body.

EPHESIANS 4:15 NIRV

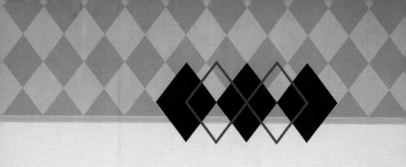

O Lord, you are true and you do not lie. You bring to pass just as you declare it, and your testimony is without deceit. If you say it, it will be so, and your Word is sure to come to pass. May I also be like you in not saying one thing and doing something else. May it be true that people trust me to follow through just as you can be trusted, so your name will be glorified. Let me speak according to the promises of your Word, which have the affirmation "yes and amen." I will not speak falsehoods as if they were true, for your Word is true.

Is there anything you need to be honest about now?

HOPE

The LORD is good to those whose hope is in him,
to the one who seeks him.

LAMENTATIONS 3:25 NIV

Hope will never bring us shame.
That's because God's love
has poured into our hearts.
This happened through the Holy Spirit,
who has been given to us.

ROMANS 5:5 NIRV

The LORD's delight is in those who fear him,
those who put their hope in his unfailing love.

PSALM 147:11 NLT

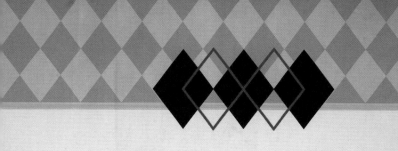

The world around me calls my attention, but my hope I put in you, O Lord. The shiny temptations of the world fade away in my eyes when I consider the promises you have established, so I will place my hope in your trustworthiness. My eyes long to see you and to experience your great kingdom. I know I won't be put to shame, but you will be pleased to give what you have promised. I humble myself before you, forsaking the things of this life, trusting in what you will bring with you in your day.

Knowing that God always hears you,
what can you be hopeful for?

HUMILITY

"Didn't I make everything by my power?
That is how all things were created," announces the Lord.
"The people I value are not proud.
They are sorry for the wrong things they have done.
They have great respect for what I say."

ISAIAH 66:2 NIRV

Humble yourselves before the Lord,
and he will lift you up.

JAMES 4:10 NIV

Pride will ruin people,
but those who are humble will be honored.

PROVERBS 29:23 NCV

My Father, I know my place—that I am your creation. I know that you value me, but I am nothing on my own. It is to you that I have value, so I humble myself before you and your goodness, trusting in you not to put me to shame. No longer will I rise up to declare what is mine, or what I deserve, because I deserve precisely what you desire to give me and only in its appropriate time. I lay myself bare before you: a mere human before his maker. I pray you will be pleased with this offering.

What opportunities have given you a chance to practice humility today?

IDENTITY

Do everything without grumbling or arguing,
so that you may become blameless and pure,
"children of God without fault
in a warped and crooked generation."
Then you will shine among them like stars in the sky
as you hold firmly to the word of life.

PHILIPPIANS 2:14-16 NIV

I have been crucified with Christ;
and it is no longer I who live,
but Christ lives in me;
and the life which I now live in the flesh
I live by faith in the Son of God,
who loved me and gave Himself up for me.

GALATIANS 2:20 NASB

My God, how marvelous it is to be called your son! To think of where I was, and how you lifted me from rebellion bolsters my love for your ways. You have shown me my humble place, and yet you lift up my head. I feel as though I could take on vast armies because of the encouragement you have given me. I will wait upon you, my Father; I will wait for your day and rejoice in the victory you take. Father, draw others also to this great gift and help me to share with my brothers the good news of your generosity and restoration.

Who do you think God really sees when he looks at you?

INSPIRATION

The precepts of the LORD are right,
giving joy to the heart.
The commands of the LORD are radiant,
giving light to the eyes.

PSALM 19:8 NIV

Your laws are my treasure;
they are my heart's delight.

PSALM 119:111 NLT

The whole Bible was given to us by inspiration from God
and is useful to teach us what is true and to make us realize
what is wrong in our lives; it straightens us out
and helps us do what is right.

2 TIMOTHY 3:16 TLB

My Lord, how majestic are your ways and how wonderful the wisdom of your Word; I desire to tell them to all the world. Your plans are right and good, and you long to see the wicked redeemed along with your people. Teach me your great wisdom and empower me to describe the wonder of your restoration to those around me. The truth of your faithfulness and grace inspire me to live righteously before you and to spread your message as you have asked.

How can you find inspiration to create something for God?

JOY

May the God of hope fill you with all joy and peace
as you trust in him, so that you may overflow with hope
by the power of the Holy Spirit.

ROMANS 15:13 NIV

"Don't be sad, because the joy of the LORD
will make you strong."

NEHEMIAH 8:10 NCV

The LORD is my strength and shield.
I trust him with all my heart.
He helps me, and my heart is filled with joy.
I burst out in songs of thanksgiving.

PSALM 28:7 NLT

Always be joyful because you belong to the Lord.
I will say it again. Be joyful!

PHILIPPIANS 4:4 NIRV

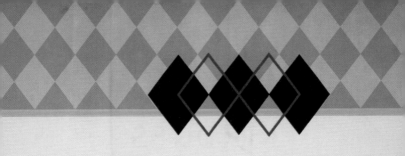

What can this life offer me compared to your great promises, O Lord? My excitement for your goodness and faithfulness is uncontainable and my heart is renewed in joy at the plans you have established for your people. My faith in your promises and Word are strengthened, and my hope in your fulfillment is assured. I cannot hold back celebrating the coming of the great King!

What is one truly joyful moment you've had recently?

KINDNESS

Be kind to each other, tenderhearted,
forgiving one another,
just as God through Christ has forgiven you.

EPHESIANS 4:32 NLT

Kind people do themselves a favor,
but cruel people bring trouble on themselves.

PROVERBS 11:17 NCV

Do you disrespect God's great kindness and favor?
Do you disrespect God when he is patient with you?
Don't you realize that God's kindness is meant
to turn you away from your sins?

ROMANS 2:4 NIRV

Great is his love toward us,
and the faithfulness of the LORD endures forever.
Praise the LORD.

PSALM 117:2 NIV

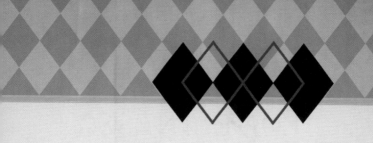

My Father, thank you for showing your kindness to me, forgiving my rebellion and sins. You are gracious to me; you extend your hand of friendship to me even though I have been your enemy. Thank you for withholding your judgment and the punishment I so rightly deserve. You have given me time to turn from my selfish ways to follow in your footsteps. Help me to be kind and forgiving to others just as you have been with me, so other people might come to know your great compassion.

How can you extend kindness to those around you today?

LONELINESS

"Teach them to obey everything that I have taught you,
and I will be with you always,
even until the end of this age."

MATTHEW 28:20 NCV

The LORD is near to all who call on him,
yes, to all who call on him in truth.

PSALM 145:18 NLT

Even if my father and mother abandon me,
the LORD will hold me close.

PSALM 27:10 NLT

"Be strong and courageous. Do not be afraid or terrified
because of them, for the LORD your God goes with you;
he will never leave you nor forsake you."

DEUTERONOMY 31:6 NIV

Father, I feel isolated and alone with no one to support me. My friends are distant and no one stands beside me. I need you now more than ever. I need a friend who sticks even closer than a brother. Surround me and support me, or I will not be able to stand. I put my hope in your Word and trust that you will not leave me. I trust that you will respond in my time of trouble, and I can rest assured that you have my back. Do not forsake me, but establish me according to your Word, and I will stand in the day of your restoration.

Can you spend time asking God to surround you with his presence now?

LOVE

Three things will last forever—
faith, hope, and love—
and the greatest of these is love.

1 CORINTHIANS 13:13 NLT

LORD, you are good. You are forgiving.
You are full of love for all who call out to you.

PSALM 86:5 NIRV

Fill us with your love every morning.
Then we will sing and rejoice all our lives.

PSALM 90:14 NCV

Let love and faithfulness never leave you;
bind them around your neck,
write them on the tablet of your heart.

PROVERBS 3:3 NIV

*Your love, my Lord, is amazing. You care for your creation
in such a marvelous way. You send the rain on all, and the
land produces food. You are patient with us, not wanting to
destroy any who might return to you. You faithfully uphold
your promises, and you stand by your people. I can have
faith, I can have hope, because your faithfulness and loving
kindness are certain. Thank you for your great love, mercy,
and grace.*

How does the love of God in your life
help you love those around you?

PATIENCE

Warn those who are lazy.
Encourage those who are timid.
Take tender care of those who are weak.
Be patient with everyone.

1 THESSALONIANS 5:14, NLT

Be like those who through faith and patience
will receive what God has promised.

HEBREWS 6:12 NCV

Be completely humble and gentle;
be patient, bearing with one another in love.

EPHESIANS 4:2 NIV

Anyone who is patient has great understanding.
But anyone who gets angry quickly
shows how foolish they are.

PROVERBS 14:29 NIRV

My Lord, I am so eager and cannot wait. I want to see things happen; I don't like the feeling of standing still. I have my plans and want to see them come about. I have my ideas of how things should be done. May your Holy Spirit fill me with the ability to wait, to be still, to trust that your ways, though they seem slow to me, are actually accomplishing your good purposes. Give me the peace of mind to wait on you and see your work happen to the glory of your name. Lord, you know I am a doer, but help me to be one who actually does your will not my own.

How can you show more patience in your daily life?

PEACE

"I have told you these things, so that you can have peace
because of me. In this world you will have trouble.
But be encouraged! I have won the battle over the world."

JOHN 16:33 NIRV

The LORD gives his people strength.
The LORD blesses them with peace.

PSALM 29:11 NLT

May the Lord of peace himself give you peace at all times
and in every way. The Lord be with all of you.

2 THESSALONIANS 3:16 NIV

"I am leaving you with a gift—peace of mind and heart.
And the peace I give is a gift the world cannot give.
So don't be troubled or afraid."

JOHN 14:27 NLT

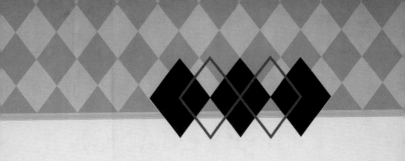

My God, the world seems to crush in around me, but I have peace in your promises and faithfulness. Relationships, pressures of life, and difficulties surround me, but you fill me with a peace that surpasses the world's understanding. Your promises are of restoration and provision, of fruitfulness and plenty, and I know that I will see those things with my own eyes. I know that in this age I will face many difficulties, and many times things will seem tight with little reprieve, but my hope is not in this age or of peace here. My hope is in you and the coming of your kingdom; therefore, I am peaceful.

What does peace look like for you?

PERSEVERANCE

In a race all the runners run.

But only one gets the prize.

You know that, don't you?

So run in a way that will get you the prize.

1 CORINTHIANS 9:24-25 NIRV

I have tried hard to find you—

don't let me wander from your commands.

PSALM 119:10 NLT

I have fought the good fight, I have finished the race,

I have kept the faith.

2 TIMOTHY 4:7 NCV

Let us not become weary in doing good,

for at the proper time

we will reap a harvest if we do not give up.

GALATIANS 6:9 NIV

Holy Spirit, I need your strength! My strength is fading as I try to finish well. I want to quit, my body is tired, and my will cries out to be satisfied. Remind me of the prize I will receive when I finish, so I may fight against the desire to settle for what I could have in this life. Encourage me by your power to see what awaits those who persevere to the end. Let me be refreshed with the fresh water of a show of your power. Strengthen me and I will finish the race, and I will give all glory to you.

What do you feel God calling you to persevere in right now?

PRAISE

Sing to the LORD a new song,

his praise from the ends of the earth,

you who go down to the sea, and all that is in it,

you islands, and all who live in them.

ISAIAH 42:10 NIV

Praise the LORD from the skies.

Praise him high above the earth.

Praise him, all you angels.

Praise him, all you armies of heaven.

Praise him, sun and moon.

Praise him, all you shining stars.

Praise him, highest heavens

and you waters above the sky.

Let them praise the LORD,

because they were created by his command.

PSALM 148:1–5 NCV

My Lord, I exalt your great name for you are the only one worthy to be praised for what has happened. You created the heavens and the earth; you ordered them and caused them to bring forth life, and you replenish them by your great strength. You judge rightly between the righteous and the wicked, and you redeem the lowly and contrite. The whole creation will be renewed, and you alone will be praised for this. I magnify you for your greatness, O God. Be pleased with this offering of praise.

What is something specific you can praise God for today?

PRAYER

LORD, in the morning you hear my voice.

In the morning I pray to you.

I wait for you in hope.

PSALM 5:3 NIRV

Never stop praying.

1 THESSALONIANS 5:17 NIRV

The LORD does not listen to the wicked,

but he hears the prayers of those who do right.

PROVERBS 15:29 NCV

Come, let us bow down in worship,

let us kneel before the LORD our Maker.

PSALM 95:6 NIV

Lord, hear my prayers, for I need you near to me. Though I long to be strong enough to face life by myself, I need your support. I need you to communicate to me the greatness of your promises and the plans you have established. I need to be able to confide in you my deficiencies and find wisdom and strength in your counsel. Show me your ways and lead me down the path that leads to life everlasting. Hear my prayers and I will be lifted up.

What can you pray about right now?

PROMISES

His divine power has granted to us everything pertaining
to life and godliness, through the true knowledge of Him
who called us by His own glory and excellence.

2 PETER 1:3-4, NASB

Your promises have been thoroughly tested,
and your servant loves them.
My eyes stay open through the watches of the night,
that I may meditate on your promises.

PSALM 119:140, 148 NIV

The LORD always keeps his promises;
he is gracious in all he does.

PSALM 145:13 NLT

All the promises of God in Him are Yes,
and in Him Amen, to the glory of God through us.

2 CORINTHIANS 1:20 NKJV

Oh, the greatness and grandeur of your promises and plans, my God! You have established them from the beginning, and you will see them come to pass; I have no doubt. Everything you have declared you also have brought to pass, delivering your people from the Egyptians, giving them the land of Israel, establishing the line of David as king, and fulfilling the promise to bring the Messiah through him. You have promised to restore the earth, to bless the nations, to put an end to famine, drought, and suffering. You will raise the dead back to life. Your past faithfulness assures us that we will indeed see you bring all of these to completeness. Blessed be the name of the Lord!

Which promises of God help you see hope in your current situation?

PROTECTION

My God is my rock. I can run to him for safety.
He is my shield and my saving strength, my defender
and my place of safety. The Lord saves me
from those who want to harm me.

2 Samuel 22:3 NCV

The Lord keeps you from all harm
and watches over your life.
The Lord keeps watch over you as you come and go,
both now and forever.

Psalm 121:7-8 NLT

The Lord is good, a refuge in times of trouble.
He cares for those who trust in him.

Nahum 1:7 NIV

Father, you are a strong tower to those who trust in you. You will not let your people be put to shame! Even though the world may gain a small victory, you will raise us back up once again. I run to you for you are worthy to be trusted, and you do not fail to provide refuge and strength. You are my protector and I am fully confident in you.

How can you lay down your battle plans and let God be your protector?

PROVISION

May he give you the power to accomplish
all the good things your faith prompts you to do.

2 Thessalonians 1:11 nlt

We are God's handiwork,
created in Christ Jesus to do good works,
which God prepared in advance for us to do.

Ephesians 2:10 niv

Just as you have always obeyed,
not as in my presence only,
but now much more in my absence,
work out your salvation
with fear and trembling;
for it is God who is at work in you,
both to will and to work for His good pleasure.

Philippians 2:12-13 nasb

Gracious Father, you provide everything I need to live and to love according to your good will. You have given me your Holy Spirit to instruct me and lead me down the path to the coming of your kingdom. You provide the refreshment and encouragement I need to travel all the way. You strengthen me to declare your good works and to rise up and join you in the work of leading others down this path. You, O Lord my God, are the source and sufficiency of all my provision. Glory be to you!

How have you seen God provide for you lately?

PURPOSE

You have been raised up with Christ.
So think about things
that are in heaven. That is where Christ is.
He is sitting at God's right hand.

COLOSSIANS 3:1 NIRV

We know that in all things God works for the good of
those who love him, who have been called according to
his purpose.

ROMANS 8:28 NIV

My child, pay attention to my words;
listen closely to what I say.
Don't ever forget my words;
keep them always in mind.

PROVERBS 4:20-21 NCV

O great King, you have established your purposes from
the very beginning of your creation. You knew what you
desired from your creation and how it was to work and be
governed. You established humanity to subdue and rule in
righteousness, according to your very image that you made us
to reflect. Lord, I pray that you will conform my will to your
will, transform my mind to reflect your thoughts, and form
my heart to care for and love your creation as you do. You
have set your Son as an example to us, may we be conformed
to his image just as he exemplified the image you had
established in the beginning, that we may all live and rule in
your kingdom as you have always purposed.

How do you feel when you think about God having a special purpose for your life?

RELATIONSHIPS

Two are better than one,
because they have a good return for their labor:
If either of them falls down,
one can help the other up.

ECCLESIASTES 4:9–10 NIV

Perfume and incense bring joy to the heart,
and the pleasantness of a friend
springs from their heartfelt advice.

PROVERBS 27:9 NIV

Love each other with genuine affection,
and take delight in honoring each other.

ROMANS 12:10 NLT

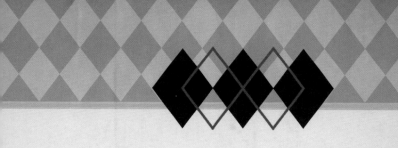

Good Father, you said in the beginning that it was not good for man to be alone, so you created a companion suitable for him with the intent to reproduce and populate the earth with many people. You desired that we live together in harmony and fellowship. Thank you for the wonderful gift of friends and families. Though these relationships rarely progress without difficulty, I acknowledge your wisdom in recognizing how good and pleasant it would be for us to fellowship with each other.

What specifically would you like to thank God for in your relationships today?

RELIABILITY

"All people are like grass. All their glory is like
the flowers in the field. The grass dries up.
The flowers fall to the ground.
But the word of the LORD lasts forever."

1 PETER 1:24-25 NIRV

Every good action and every perfect gift is from God.
These good gifts come down from the Creator of the sun,
moon, and stars, who does not change like their
shifting shadows.

JAMES 1:17 NCV

You are near, LORD,
and all your commands are true.
Long ago I learned from your statutes
that you established them to last forever.

PSALM 119:151-152 NIV

My good and gracious God, creator of the heavens and the earth, you have set your Word in granite, and it will not be shaken. You are faithful and true to your will, and you make it come to pass. You created the universe in grandeur and called it very good; you intend to keep it in place by the strength of your might. I know that I can trust in you and you will not let me fall; I can put my hope in you, and you are reliable to sustain and support me. By your Holy Spirit, and according to your promises, make me to be an imitator of your reliability in all that I say and do.

How does it make you feel knowing you can rely on God for everything?

RESPECT

Show respect for all people: Love the brothers
and sisters of God's family, respect God, honor the king.

1 PETER 2:17 NCV

Trust in your leaders.
Put yourselves under their authority.
Do this, because they keep watch over you.
They know they are
accountable to God for everything they do.
Do this, so that their work will be a joy.
If you make their work a heavy load,
it won't do you any good.

HEBREWS 13:17 NIRV

Don't do anything only to get ahead. Don't do it
because you are proud. Instead, be humble.
Value others more than yourselves.

PHILIPPIANS 2:3 NIRV

My Lord, mold me into a person who does not think too highly of myself, but who respects the validity of other people. Help me to see others as highly valuable and not to see myself as better than they are. Help me to maintain a humble attitude and to treat others with the respect they deserve, not only because they are respectable but also because they are made in your image. Be magnified, Lord, and honored among all humanity.

How can you show respect to God?

RESTORATION

He has saved us and called us to a holy life—
not because of anything we have done but because
of his own purpose and grace.

2 TIMOTHY 1:9 NIV

Since we have been made right in God's sight by faith,
we have peace with God because of what Jesus Christ
our Lord has done for us. Because of our faith,
Christ has brought us into this place of undeserved
privilege where we now stand, and we confidently and
joyfully look forward to sharing God's glory.

ROMANS 5:1–2 NLT

"Let us praise the Lord, the God of Israel,
because he has come to help his people
and has given them freedom.
He has given us a powerful Savior."

LUKE 1:68-69 NCV

Almighty King, from the earliest of your promises to humanity that you would send a Son who would crush the authority of the devil, restoration has been in your heart. All of human history has been the story of you working to bring about your promised redemption, and your creation longs to be restored to its pre-curse state. Humanity cries out to be made new and to stand in fellowship and confidence before its great king and creator. Father, I pray as my Savior did, that your kingdom come, and that your will finally be done here on earth as it is done in heaven.

Have you experienced the power of restoration in your life?

REWARD

Work willingly at whatever you do, as though you were
working for the Lord rather than for people. Remember
that the Lord will give you an inheritance as your reward,
and that the Master you are serving is Christ.

COLOSSIANS 3:23-24 NLT

"Love your enemies, do good to them,
and lend to them without expecting to get anything back.
Then your reward will be great,
and you will be children of the Most High,
because he is kind to the ungrateful and wicked."

LUKE 6:35 NIV

Without faith it is impossible to please God.
Those who come to God must believe that he exists.
And they must believe
that he rewards those who look to him.

HEBREWS 11:6 NIRV

O my God, the source of my joy and happiness, let my hope be set fully on you and the salvation you bring with you to reward those who have diligently and earnestly sought you! Let me not serve or act in this life for the short-sighted benefits. The everlasting reward of your grace and favor are like the rarest gemstones in comparison. I look to you and your reward and glory in the benefit you have promised to bestow in the day of your coming.

How does it make you feel knowing that God will reward you for your diligence?

SAFETY

The LORD also will be a refuge for the oppressed,
A refuge in times of trouble.
Those who know Your name will put their trust in You;
For You, LORD, have not forsaken those who seek You.

PSALM 9:9–10 NKJV

The name of the LORD is a strong tower;
The righteous runs into it and is safe.

PROVERBS 18:10 NASB

Wherever I am, though far away at the ends of the earth,
I will cry to you for help.
When my heart is faint and overwhelmed,
lead me to the mighty, towering Rock of safety.
For you are my refuge,
a high tower where my enemies can never reach me.

PSALM 61:2-3 TLB

My Savior and King, I know that you are my refuge from the storms of life that beat and crash against me. You sustain me and keep me safe against the attacks of the enemy who wishes to see me falter and fail to attain the goal of your promised restoration. When no one else is able to provide support, you are my true rock of safety. Support me now, for I am tired and weary from the struggle. I need your rest, and I reside in your safety.

Do you feel safe when you think about God being near you?

SALVATION

"This is how God loved the world:
He gave his one and only Son,
so that everyone who believes in him will not perish
but have eternal life."

JOHN 3:16 NLT

The wages of sin is death, but the gift of God
is eternal life in Christ Jesus our Lord.

ROMANS 6:23 NIV

God's grace has saved you because of your faith in Christ.
Your salvation doesn't come from anything you do.
It is God's gift.

EPHESIANS 2:8 NIRV

If you openly declare that Jesus is Lord and believe in your
heart that God raised him from the dead, you will be saved.

ROMANS 10:9 NLT

Father, I await your salvation from on high. You have promised it, and you are faithful to all of your promises. From the very beginning you have promised the salvation of the world, and through Jesus the Messiah, you have assured it. I know that you are faithful to your promise to restore and resurrect because I know that your Son sits at your right hand awaiting the day you send him to restore breath to my failing body and raise me to everlasting life. I long for this anticipated salvation to come and am refreshed in joy and peace at the assurance you have given me through the cross that Jesus bore.

How do you respond to the message of salvation?

SATISFACTION

Because your love is better than life,
my lips will glorify you.
I will praise you as long as I live,
and in your name I will lift up my hands.
I will be fully satisfied as with the richest of foods;
with singing lips my mouth will praise you.

PSALM 63:3–5 NIV

The LORD is all I need.
He takes care of me.
My share in life has been pleasant;
my part has been beautiful.

PSALM 16:5–6 NCV

The poor shall eat and be satisfied; all who see the Lord
shall find him and shall praise his name.
Their hearts shall rejoice with everlasting joy.

PSALM 22:26 TLB

Father, my heart praises you for you have filled me to overflowing; you have overwhelmed me with what you have decreed. Like Abraham who was amazed at the promises you made to him, I am filled with awe at your goodness. I am satisfied with your gifts, and my heart is not interested in what the world has to offer. Thank you for your generosity and love.

Are you satisfied with all God has given you?

SERVING

Each of you should use whatever gift you have received
to serve others, as faithful stewards of God's grace in its
various forms. If anyone serves, they should do so with
the strength God provides, so that in all things God may
be praised through Jesus Christ.

1 PETER 4:10-11 NIV

Always give yourselves fully to the work of the Lord,
because you know that your labor in the Lord
is not in vain.

1 CORINTHIANS 15:58 NIV

You were called to freedom.
Do not use your freedom
as an opportunity for the flesh,
but through love serve one another.

GALATIANS 5:13 ESV

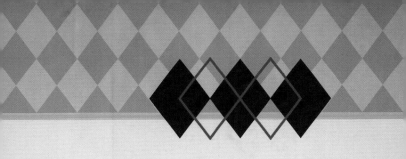

Lord, I can hardly fathom the depths of your goodness. You have said that the greatest among us shall be the servant of all. This is your great gift to each of us, for in the day of your greatest glory you will take up your place to delight in serving your people. You are not so proud to remain aloft, but instead, you come down to me and make your place with me. Lord, fill me with this same heart of service that I may follow your example. May I be humble like you and serve others with all of my heart.

How can you serve God and others today?

STRENGTH

God is our refuge and strength,
an ever-present help in trouble.

PSALM 46:1-3 NIV

The Lord is faithful; he will strengthen you
and guard you from the evil one.

2 THESSALONIANS 3:3 NIRV

"Don't be afraid, for I am with you.
Don't be discouraged, for I am your God.
I will strengthen you and help you.
I will hold you up with my victorious right hand."

ISAIAH 41:10 NLT

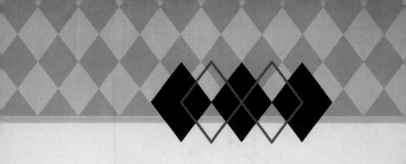

You have strengthened me with your Spirit of truth, God, and have not abandoned me in my time of need. Temptation presents itself before me, yet you have placed your shield before me, and I taste victory in the battle against the enemy of my soul. You are my strong tower and my guard, and though I am weak myself, in my weakness you show yourself to be strong. I trust in you and magnify your rule. You are good and gracious in all your ways!

In what areas do you need God to be your strength today?

STRESS

Praise the LORD, my soul;
all my inmost being, praise his holy name.
Praise the LORD, my soul,
and forget not all his benefits—
who forgives all your sins
and heals all your diseases,
who redeems your life from the pit
and crowns you with love and compassion,
who satisfies your desires with good things
so that your youth is renewed like the eagle's.

PSALM 103:1-5 NIV

Commit your actions to the LORD.
and your plans will succeed.

PROVERBS 16:3 NLT

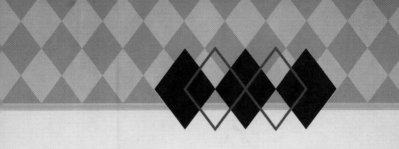

My Father, you are the source of peace and comfort. While in this world I have trouble and many things stress me mentally and physically, you have promised an end to the trials. You will heal, you will restore, you will forgive, you will satisfy hunger and thirst. Father, direct my path to come in line with the promises you have made; help me to walk in that path, and even when trials come, I will rest assured that they will not overcome me. Indeed, I will eat at your table in your kingdom.

When was the last time you were able to let go of stress and just sit with God?

SUPPORT

Whom have I in heaven but you?
And earth has nothing I desire besides you.
My flesh and my heart may fail,
but God is the strength of my heart
and my portion forever.

PSALM 73:25–26 NIV

You, God, see the trouble of the afflicted;
you consider their grief and take it in hand.
The victims commit themselves to you;
you are the helper of the fatherless.

PSALM 10:14 NIV

You are my hiding place;
You shall preserve me from trouble;
You shall surround me with songs of deliverance.

PSALM 32:7 NKJV

Gracious God, you are a help to the helpless and a support to the weak. You assist those in trouble, and your heart draws near the humble and contrite. You will not let them be put to shame but will vindicate them and raise them up in the day of your coming. Father, I need your support and help. Everything within me cries out to stand on my own two feet and overcome through my own strength, but that has only led me to greater difficulty and grief. Humbly I ask for your help to act rightly and to love well, to support the weak, and to defend the helpless. Give the support I need to bear up under pressure and to assist my brothers in their time of need.

When do you feel most supported by God?

SUSTENANCE

God is able to bless you abundantly,
so that in all things
at all times, having all that you need,
you will abound in every good work.

2 CORINTHIANS 9:8 NIV

The LORD is my shepherd, I shall not want.
He makes me lie down in green pastures;
he leads me beside still waters;
he restores my soul.

PSALM 23:1–3 NRSV

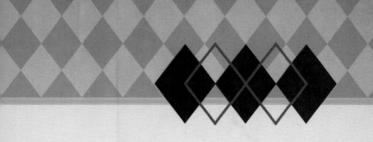

O God, you have created all things and you sustain them in their places by the force of your will. I put my trust in you as you are the source from which I receive all good things, including the necessities of life. Sustain me by your great power and by your Holy Spirit that I might continue in the course of life. I know that your plans are for great abundance to be poured out on the earth, and that you withhold now from fully fulfilling that desire in order to draw more people to you. While I wait, do not forget those who place their hope in you. Give me each day my daily bread, and I will praise you with great adoration in the day of your kingdom.

How do you get your sustenance from God?

TRUST

Those who know the LORD trust him,
because he will not leave those who come to him.

PSALM 9:10 NCV

I trust in you, LORD. I say, "You are my God."
My whole life is in your hands.
Save me from the hands of my enemies.
Save me from those who are chasing me.

PSALM 31:14-15 NIV

Yes, the LORD is for me; he will help me.
I will look in triumph at those who hate me.
It is better to take refuge in the LORD
than to trust in people.

PSALM 118:7-8 NLT

Lord, you are a keeper of promises. When you say you will do something, you make sure to fulfill your word. I have seen you follow through in my own life in many ways. Anyone who puts their trust in you will not be disappointed, and I will trust you with my life. You will restore your people and give them great blessing in the day of your visitation so that even when you call me to the ultimate testimony of faith, I will have nothing to fear, for I trust in you.

How do you know that God is trustworthy?

TRUTH

"When he, the Spirit of truth, comes,
he will guide you into all the truth."

JOHN 16:13 NIV

The very essence of your words is truth;
all your just regulations will stand forever.

PSALM 119:160 NLT

"If you abide in My word,
you are My disciples indeed.
And you shall know the truth,
and the truth shall make you free."

JOHN 8:31-32 NKJV

Teach me your way, O LORD,
that I may walk in your truth;
unite my heart to fear your name.

PSALM 86:11 ESV

O God, you are the source of all truth; all other sources have changed the truth for some form of a lie. I will believe your Word. Your plans continue to come true, and you thwart the plans of your enemies. Just as in the trials of Egypt, what you have decreed happens, and your adversaries are ashamed. In the coming days, many words will go forth and many will testify wrongly about the circumstances of the day, but your Word will stand out as true, and your people will be vindicated for believing in you.

What steps can you take to incorporate God's truth in your life?

UNDERSTANDING

Understanding is like a fountain of life
to those who have it.
But foolish people are punished
for the foolish things they do.

PROVERBS 16:22 NIRV

The teaching of your word gives light,
so even the simple can understand.

PSALM 119:130 NLT

Give me understanding,
so that I may keep your law and obey it with all my heart.

PSALM 119:34 NIV

Don't act thoughtlessly,
but understand what the Lord wants you to do.

EPHESIANS 5:17 NLT

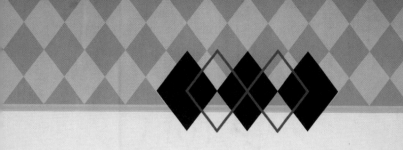

My Lord, you have said that your ways are not mine, and your thoughts are dramatically different than my own. How then might I understand your ways? Search my heart, God, and see that I desire to understand your truth. Teach me by your Holy Spirit and Word the ways you have set forth so I may walk according to them. I pray for your light on my path so I may obey you in all ways.

How do you seek to understand God's will?

VICTORY

You can prepare a horse for the day of battle.
But the power to win comes from the LORD.

PROVERBS 21:31 NIRV

Every child of God defeats this evil world,
and we achieve this victory through our faith.

1 JOHN 5:4 NLT

From the LORD comes deliverance.
May your blessing be on your people.

PSALM 3:8 NIV

"The LORD your God is the one who goes with you
to fight for you against your enemies to give you victory."

DEUTERONOMY 20:4 NIV

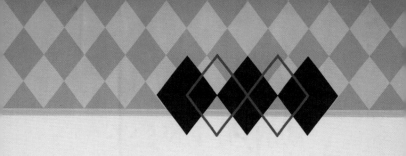

O my King and Father, how glorious are you in your ways. You have made yourself ready for battle on behalf of your people, and they will be vindicated in the eyes of the world. Your plans have been made known since the beginning, yet your enemies are powerless to thwart you. I magnify your name, giving glory to you for the great triumph you have established by the cross of Jesus the Messiah. Bring to fullness this victory and a joyful noise will rise from your people to your great glory.

What was the last victory you experienced?

WHOLENESS

He will take our weak mortal bodies and change them
into glorious bodies like his own, using the same power
with which he will bring everything under his control.

PHILIPPIANS 3:21 NLT

Celebrate with praises the God and Father of our Lord
Jesus Christ, who has shown us his extravagant mercy.
For his fountain of mercy has given us a new life—we are
reborn to experience a living, energetic hope through
the resurrection of Jesus Christ from the dead. We are
reborn into a perfect inheritance that can never perish,
never be defiled, and never diminish. It is promised
and preserved forever in the heavenly realm for you!
Through our faith, the mighty power of God constantly
guards us until our full salvation is ready to be
revealed in the last time.

1 PETER 1:3–5 TPT

Father, creation groans in longing for the revealing your glory on the day of resurrection. In that day, all creation will be made whole. Your people will govern the earth in righteousness, and healing will flow from your throne to all the world. In that day, the earth will no longer experience drought or famine, the poor will be well fed, and the righteous dead will finally receive their promised inheritance in life. Hallelujah to you, my great King, who makes whole your creation that has been subjected to futility! Your name will be praised for everlasting days.

How does understanding eternal wholeness benefit you in this life?

WISDOM

Wisdom will come into your mind,
and knowledge will be pleasing to you.
Good sense will protect you;
understanding will guard you
It will keep you from the wicked,
from those whose words are bad.

PROVERBS 2:10-12 NCV

Wisdom and money can get you almost anything,
but only wisdom can save your life.

ECCLESIASTES 7:12 NLT

If any of you needs wisdom, you should ask God for it.
He will give it to you. God gives freely to everyone
and doesn't find fault.

JAMES 1:5 NIRV

Father, I ask by your Holy Spirit for your wisdom that lights the path of the righteous. Fill me with your understanding and insight into life and faith. Help me by your teaching to live wisely in these days, and I will be raised on the great day of the Lord to give glory and honor to you. Magnify your name among your people according to your great wisdom and skill, and the glory of your throne will shine forevermore.

What can you ask for God's wisdom in today?

WORRY

Turn your worries over to the LORD.
He will keep you going.
He will never let godly people be shaken.

PSALM 55:22 NIRV

"Who of you by worrying can add a single hour to your life?"

LUKE 12:25 NIV

Worry weighs a person down;
an encouraging word cheers a person up.

PROVERBS 12:25 NLT

Do not worry about anything, but pray and ask God
for everything you need, always giving thanks.
And God's peace,
which is so great we cannot understand it,
will keep your hearts and minds in Christ Jesus.

PHILIPPIANS 4:6-7 NCV

Heavenly Father, I give you my worries and cares, for you are able to take them and fulfill my needs. You are powerful with great wealth, and you have promised to sustain and restore those who have put their trust in you. I believe in your great promises and place my trust in you, putting my hope in the fulfillment of your will. I magnify your name and your great love and faithfulness, and I will reside in peace in the blessing of your beautiful kingdom. What more have I to fear in the care of the great King?

What worries can you hand over to God today?

BroadStreet Publishing Group, LLC.
Savage, Minnesota, USA
Broadstreetpublishing.com

Prayers & Promises for Men

978-1-4245-6465-1
978-1-4245-6062-2 (ebook)

Prayers composed by D. E. Gregory.